T0387387

The Revolutionary War

by Daniel R. Faust

Consultant: Caitlin Krieck
Social Studies Teacher and Instructional Coach
The Lab School of Washington

BEARPORT
PUBLISHING

Minneapolis, Minnesota

Credits

Cover and title page, © flysnowfly/Shutterstock; 4–5, © Gino Santa Maria/Shutterstock; 8, © Library of Congress/Wikimedia Creative Commons license 3.0; 9, © GL Archive/Alamy; 12–13, © Science History Images/Alamy; 11, © Photos.com/Getty Images; 13, © John Singleton Copley/Wikimedia Creative Commons license 3.0; 15, © Nastasic/iStock; 17, © Pyty/Shutterstock; 19, © Andrea Izzotti/Shutterstock; 21, © Domenick D'Andrea/Wikimedia Creative Commons license 3.0; 22–23, © New York Public Library/Wikimedia Creative Commons license 3.0; 25, © Library of Congress/Wikimedia Creative Commons license 3.0; 27, © Orhan Cam/Shutterstock; and 28, © Anadolu_Dizgi/Shutterstock.

Bearport Publishing Company Product Development Team

President: Jen Jenson; Director of Product Development: Spencer Brinker; Managing Editor: Allison Juda; Associate Editor: Naomi Reich; Associate Editor: Tiana Tran; Senior Designer: Colin O'Dea; Associate Designer: Elena Klinkner; Associate Designer: Kayla Eggert; Product Development Specialist: Anita Stasson

A NOTE FROM THE PUBLISHER: Some of the historic photos in this book have been colorized to help readers have a more meaningful and rich experience. The color results are not intended to depict actual historical detail.

Library of Congress Cataloging-in-Publication Data

Names: Faust, Daniel R., author.
Title: The Revolutionary War / by Daniel R. Faust ; consultant, Caitlin Krieck.
Description: Minneapolis, Minnesota : Bearport Publishing, 2023. | Series: U.S. history: need to know | Includes bibliographical references and index.
Identifiers: LCCN 2023006495 (print) | LCCN 2023006496 (ebook) | ISBN 9798888220320 (library binding) | ISBN 9798888222232 (paperback) | ISBN 9798888223475 (ebook)
Subjects: LCSH: United States—History—Revolution, 1775-1783—Juvenile literature.
Classification: LCC E208 .F38 2023 (print) | LCC E208 (ebook) | DDC 973.3—dc23/eng/20230223
LC record available at https://lccn.loc.gov/2023006495
LC ebook record available at https://lccn.loc.gov/2023006496

For more information, write to Bearport Publishing, 5357 Penn Avenue South, Minneapolis, MN 55419.

Contents

Fireworks and Flags

Have you ever been to a Fourth of July picnic? Maybe your city has a parade or a fireworks show. What's so special about this day? July 4th is known as **Independence** Day in the United States. This day celebrates the **founding** of the country.

Becoming the United States was not easy. It took many years of fighting a war. This came to be known as the War of Independence or the Revolutionary War.

The First Thirteen

The United States started as 13 **colonies**. These were like small states with local governments. They had to listen to the bigger British government, too.

People in the colonies were called colonists. Some were angry they had to follow British laws. They wanted more say in what happened to them.

Some British laws were about taxes. The colonists had to pay extra money when they bought certain things. There were colonists who thought the taxes were too high.

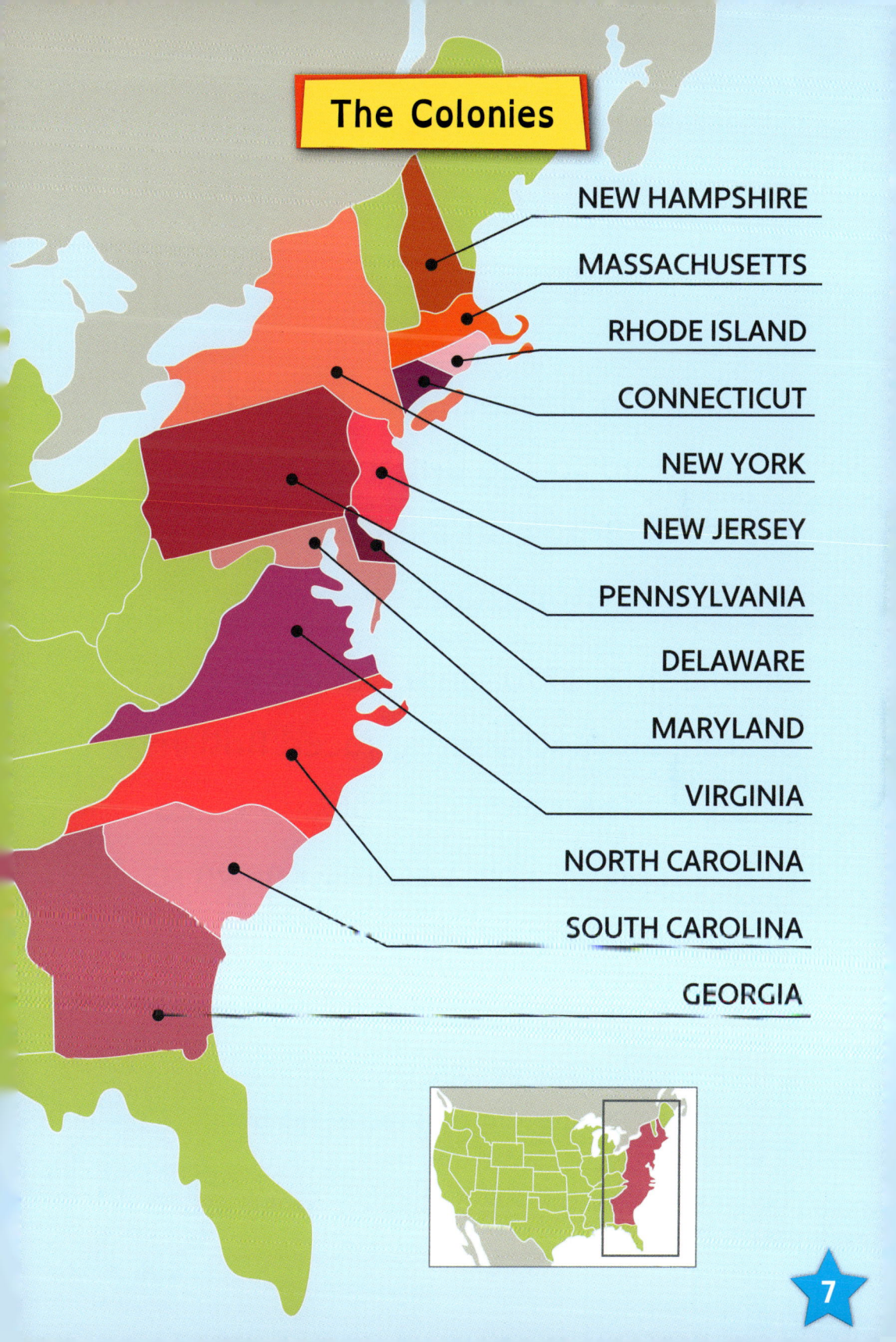

The Colonies

NEW HAMPSHIRE

MASSACHUSETTS

RHODE ISLAND

CONNECTICUT

NEW YORK

NEW JERSEY

PENNSYLVANIA

DELAWARE

MARYLAND

VIRGINIA

NORTH CAROLINA

SOUTH CAROLINA

GEORGIA

It Begins in Boston

Colonists in Massachusetts decided to stand up to the British. They had **protests**. Britain's King George III sent soldiers to stop them.

On March 5, 1770, angry colonists in Boston, Massachusetts, faced British soldiers. The soldiers shot and killed five colonists. This became known as the Boston Massacre.

Crispus Attucks was the first colonist killed during the massacre. He is often considered the first person to die in the Revolutionary War.

8

The Boston Massacre

The relationship between the British and the colonists grew worse. Eventually, the British took over the local government in Boston. They passed more laws to punish the colonists. But that backfired. Colonists made another government in Concord, Massachusetts. Soon, people in the other colonies joined the cause.

Angry colonists refused to buy things from Great Britain. A group of colonists destroyed British tea on a ship in Boston Harbor. The event came to be called the Boston Tea Party.

The Boston
Tea Party

11

The British Are Coming!

British soldiers were sent to arrest colonial leaders in Concord. But the colonists found out and went to stop the British. The two sides met near the towns of Lexington and Concord on April 19, 1775. The Revolutionary War officially began.

12

A group of colonists rode horses through the night to warn others that the British were coming. Paul Revere was one of these famous riders.

Army vs. Army

The colonies did not have a big army before the war. As the fighting picked up, they formed the Continental Army. Those joining the fight called themselves **patriots**.

Soon, the patriots and the British clashed again. The British won the Battle of Bunker Hill. Still, the battle showed that the colonists were a threat.

> The Battle of Bunker Hill lasted only two hours, but many died. More than 1,000 of the 2,400 British soldiers were killed. About 500 of the 1,800 patriot fighters were killed, hurt, or caught.

The Battle of Bunker Hill was two months after Lexington and Concord.

15

The British army was larger and had more training than the patriots. They won many of the early battles in the Revolutionary War. But the British had one major disadvantage. The army had to wait for orders and supplies to cross the Atlantic Ocean.

Great Britain is more than 3,000 miles (4,800 km) from North America. During the Revolutionary War, it could take more than six weeks to cross the Atlantic Ocean.

Great Britain

The Colonies

ATLANTIC OCEAN

N
W   E
S

17

From Colonies to States

As the nation battled, **representatives** from the 13 colonies met in Philadelphia, Pennsylvania. They decided they were no longer ruled by Great Britain. The 13 colonies became independent states. On July 4, 1776, they signed the Declaration of Independence to make it official.

The Declaration of Independence was written by Thomas Jefferson. It listed the reasons the colonies had gone to war. One of the big ones was that the colonists wanted to govern themselves.

IN CONGRESS

The unanimous Declaration of the thirtee

19

The Fight for New York

The patriots took Boston back from the British in 1776. A few months later, the Continental Army lost the Battle of Long Island near New York City. After this battle, the British army took control of New York City. The British would control the city for the rest of the war.

Boston and New York City were **port** cities. Both sides wanted to control ports. Ships could deliver goods to these cities. Soldiers, food, and equipment all traveled by ship.

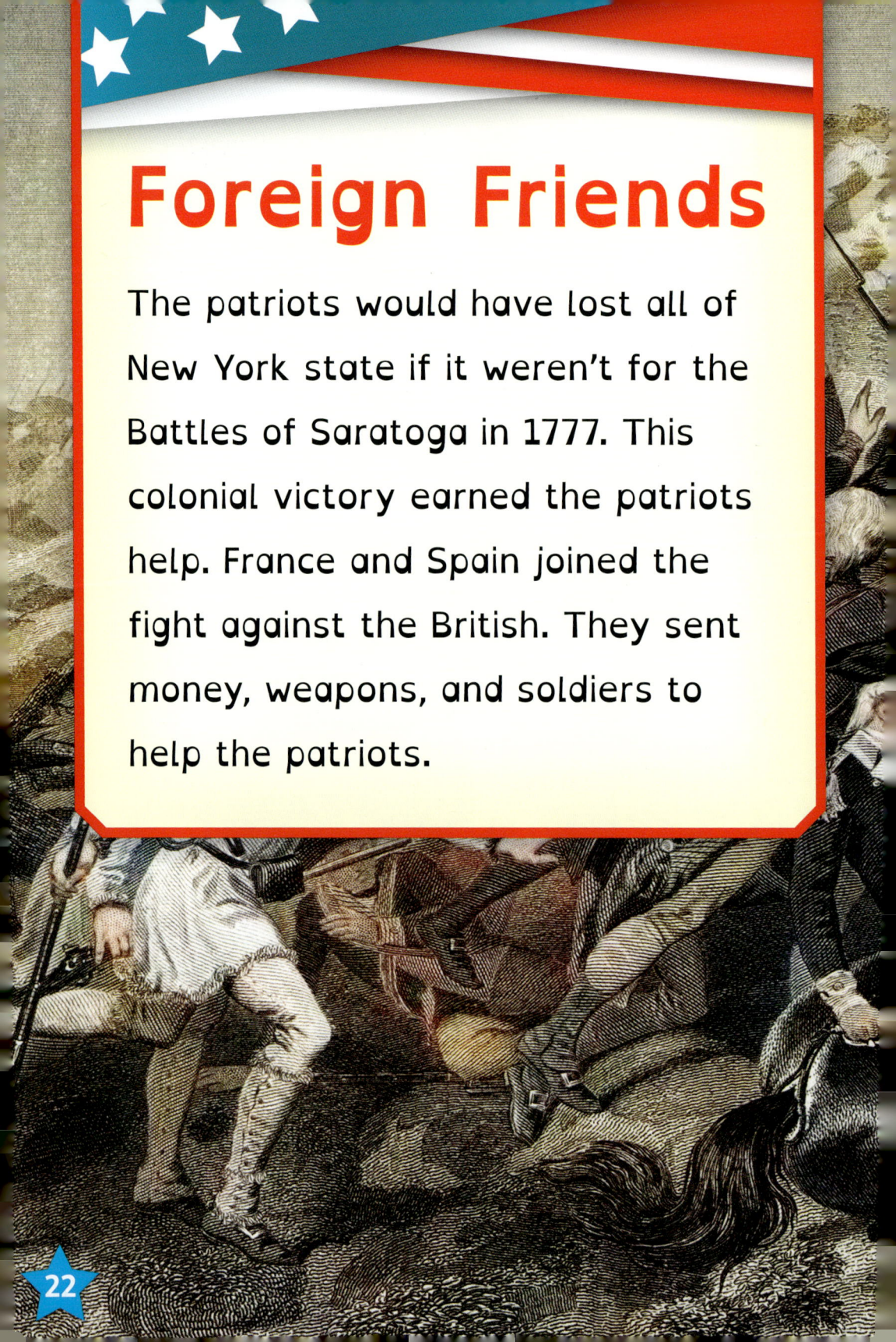

Foreign Friends

The patriots would have lost all of New York state if it weren't for the Battles of Saratoga in 1777. This colonial victory earned the patriots help. France and Spain joined the fight against the British. They sent money, weapons, and soldiers to help the patriots.

When France and Spain joined, the Revolutionary War became a world war. Great Britain had to send soldiers to fight France and Spain in other places. There were battles in India and Africa.

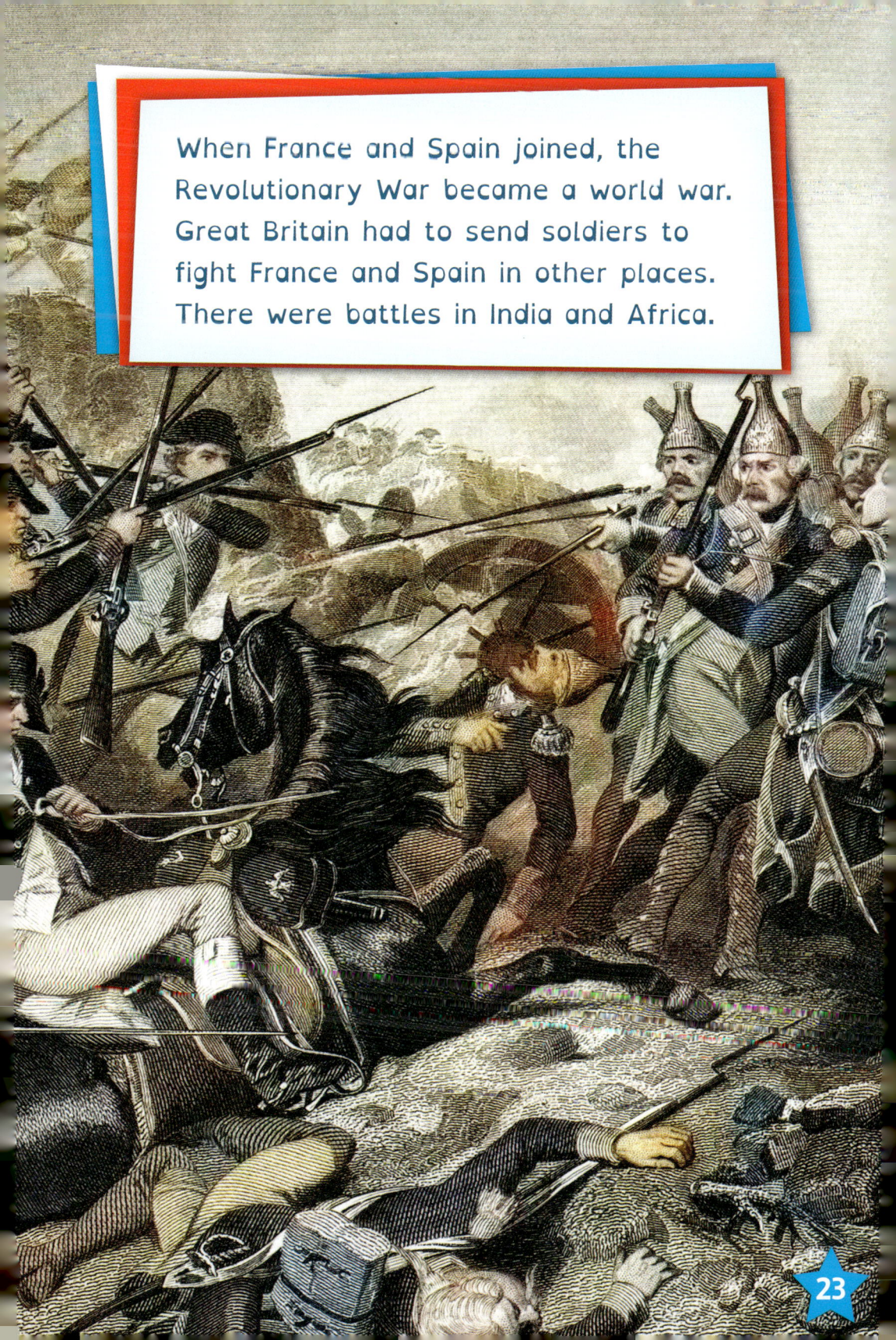

The War Ends

With France's help, the patriots surrounded the British army at the Battle of Yorktown. The British were outnumbered. They **surrendered** to the patriots. It was the final battle of the war.

Years later, the **Treaty** of Paris officially ended the war. It made the United States of America an independent country.

The British army surrendered to General George Washington. Washington earned great respect during the war. He later became the first president of the United States.

George Washington (*right*) led the colonists during the war.

Something New

The hard-fought Revolutionary War led to a new country. It was one unlike any other in the world. The United States made a new kind of government. Its people chose their leaders. It's the same kind of government still in place in the United States and around the globe today.

The Revolutionary War inspired others to stand up to their leaders. Soon, people in France, Latin America, the Caribbean, and Ireland also fought for independence.

Places of the Revolutionary War

Review the key places in America's war for independence.

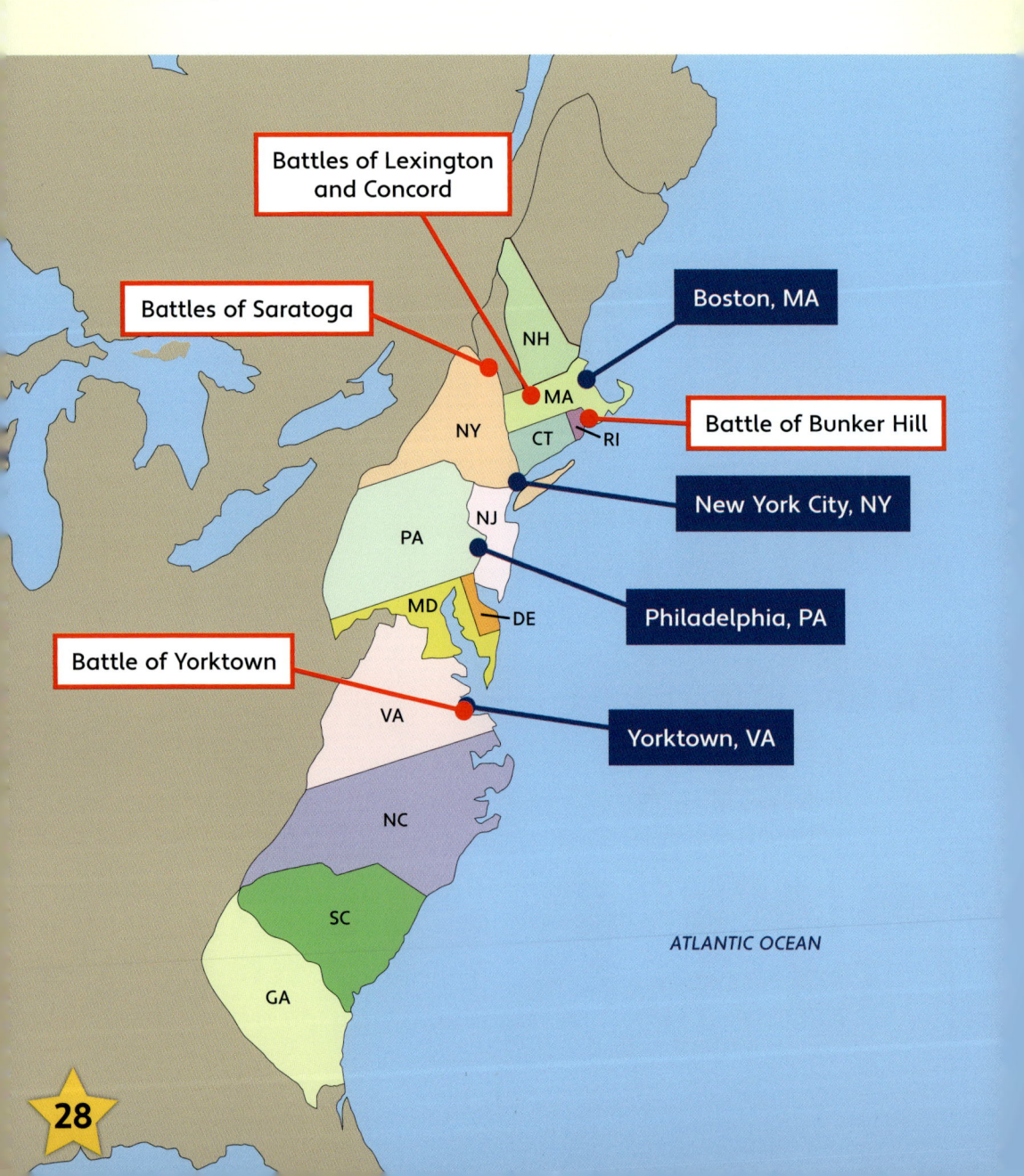

Battles of Lexington and Concord

Battles of Saratoga

Boston, MA

Battle of Bunker Hill

New York City, NY

Philadelphia, PA

Battle of Yorktown

Yorktown, VA

NH
MA
NY
CT
RI
PA
NJ
MD
DE
VA
NC
SC
GA

ATLANTIC OCEAN

★ SilverTips for REVIEW

Review what you've learned. Use the text to help you.

Define key terms

colonies

Declaration of
   Independence

patriots

representatives

Treaty of Paris

Check for understanding

Why were some of the colonists angry at Great Britain?

What was the purpose of the Declaration of Independence?

How did the Battles of Saratoga change the war for the patriots?

Think deeper

How would your life be different if the Revolutionary War never happened?

★ SilverTips on TEST-TAKING

- **Make a study plan.** Ask your teacher what the test is going to cover. Then, set aside time to study a little bit every day.

- **Read all the questions carefully.** Be sure you know what is being asked.

- **Skip any questions** you don't know how to answer right away. Mark them and come back later if you have time.

Glossary

colonies areas that have been settled by people from another country and are ruled by that original country

independence freedom from outside control

patriots the name the colonists gave themselves during the Revolutionary War

port a place where ships can stop to load or unload

protests demonstrations against things people think are wrong

representatives people who have been chosen to speak for larger groups

surrendered gave up on something, such as a war

treaty an agreement between two or more countries or groups

Read More

Abramson, Marcia. *The Declaration of Independence (X-treme Facts: History).* Minneapolis: Bearport Publishing Company, 2021.

Gagne, Tammy. *Fact and Fiction of the American Revolution (Fact and Fiction of American History).* Minneapolis: Abdo Publishing, 2022.

Gunderson, Jessica. *Sybil Ludington Rides to the Rescue: Courageous Kid of the American Revolution (Courageous Kids).* North Mankato, MN: Capstone Press, 2021.

Learn More Online

1. Go to **www.factsurfer.com** or scan the QR code below.

2. Enter "**Revolutionary War**" into the search box.

3. Click on the cover of this book to see a list of websites.

31

Index

About the Author

Daniel R. Faust is a freelance writer of fiction and nonfiction. He lives in Brooklyn, NY.